Beyond The Call of Beauty

Beyond The Call of Beauty

By

James Murphy

Published by Avalanche

Copyright James Murphy 2007 All rights reserved

No part of this book may be reproduced. Stored in a retrieval system, or transmitted by any means without the written permission of the author.

First published by Avalanche 08/23/2007

ISBN: 978-0-9556799-0-2

Found in a Humidor & Where the Silent Ones Speak
by kind permission of Carol Lynn Stevenson Grellas.

Acknowledgements

To my wife Fiona, Who suffered my long absences at the keyboard.
Julie, for having the stamina to read everything I came up with.
Carol Lynn, for acting as my unpaid editor and inspiration.
Marilyn, for all her help with the final layout.
I would also like to thank all of my fellow writers at The Critical Poet and Creative Writers for their kindness and support.
Oh, and Paddy for the Journey, God bless.

5.30am	1
Things I mislaid	2
Things to Do When We Sleep	3
I Took A Long Time To Lose You	4
Observations From The Barber Shop	5
Smile	6
The Canadian Solution	7
I Read The Eulogy At Your Final Gathering	8
All We Are Is A Broken Promise	9
Caught Inciting Poetry	10
Distance	11
Envelope worker sealed his own fate	12
Right Of Way	13
Resurgence	14
Something Stalks Me In The Dark	15
Where The Silent Ones Speak	16
Savages	18
Leonard Said	19
Martha Said	20
Old Friend	21
Just One A day	22

Thoughts On Love, And Other Things	23
Pigeons	24
Winter	25
Ticking Clocks	26
One Legged Man	27
Hope	28
How Long Shall I Kneel	29
The Devils Excuse Me	30
Cords	31
Broken Scissors	32
Unfinished Work	33
So Softly Falls The Dust Again	34
You Showed To Me The Blackest Rose	35
Monday Night Is Dungeon Night	36
Let Us Turn Our Life Down Low	37
His Ambiguous Writings On Love	38
Changes	39
Death Of A Wish	40
Lady Of The Flame Red Hair	41
No Need To Feel Bad	42
The Gift	43
The Tales My Father Told	44

Jewels	45
Did You Find Your Christmas?	46
I Poet	47
Jeanne d'Arc	48
Do Not Worry, Just For Today	49
Found In A Humidor	50
Cheap Tricks	52
One Day I Will Write	53
A Little Laid Back	54
A Discourse On Writing Implements, And Lust	55
Alone But Never Lonely	56
The Ambiguity Of Descent	56
Buddha Days	57
I Always Thought Your Eyes were Lovely	58
I Struggled With Greed	59
You Call Again My frequent Friend	60
Oblivion	61
We Try, My Love	62
Today I Wore My Sunday Face	63
In Between Nowhere	64
An Unexpected Turn Of Phrase	65
Confession Rips The Heart Asunder	66

Aphrodite Gives The Game Away	67
Not Really a Fairytale	68
Perhaps A Morsel Of Truth	69
We All Should Be So Cursed	70
You Know I Love You	71
Torquemada Lay Down Your Burning Effigy	72
Say what you like	73
If I Never See You Again	74
Do You Have A Moment?	75
Paddy's Rocket	76
The Mutterings Of A Distressed Poet	77
Dark Fantasies	78

5.30am
The morning has a brand new smell,
as I step into this empty portrait of love.
Birds consider their song, but are they really
in any rush to disturb this rare peace?
Everything is still, even the breeze
is idle, but as I listen, the gears of time
push hard upon the day.

7.00am
The railway station draws in the first
of my comrades. Yet they move
with jerky uncertainty, as if unsure of
their own requirements.
Coffee? Newspaper? Or just sit quietly
and watch the streaming schedule of
life in transit.

7.55am
The train pulls in, as if moving through
liquid, forcing its way to the platform.
Lady Julie said, I never travel unless it's
first class, but she has always had that
eye for the opulent.
But today I am not the driver of my
destiny, and I suspect my ticket is for
one ride to many.

Things I mislaid

I found understanding
on the Internet, but shunned
the fashion Buddhists,
when they sent out for vegetarian
lasagne, while meditating with
knees knotted to remind them
Of their piety.

I found darkness
in a bitter old well, where I would
visit frequently to draw from
its purity, and wallow in the
self satisfaction of my own
sacrifices.

I found wisdom
in a well leafed Readers Digest,
while waiting to see how many
points I had scored,
and if suicide was still not
an option.

I found my strength of character
where it had always been.

Things to Do When We Sleep

Ten thousand words
fell to earth,
blazing like sun's.
Each carried
a prophetic vision,
that scorched
my conscious,
and remained
late into the day.

Then I became
the little Buddha,
sitting without
distraction.
My perversions
unbridled,
my demands
exacting,
my thoughts...

Controlled?

I Took A Long Time To Lose You

I took a long time to lose you
So you would never fall
To pain and ill diversity
I passed to one and all

I took a long time to love you
But left the best unsaid
To you who wanted sanctuary
And you who needed bread

I took a long time to hold you
Though could not stand to see
The way in which you wanted love
Or how love wanted me

I took a long time to find you
Then lost the thought to give
You everything she took from me
But not the thought to live

I took a long time to kiss you
Yet lips must never spill
The guilty longing in my soul
That's longing for you still

Observations From The Barber Shop

So we brokered no thoughts of desertion
When the prophets confessed to their fraud
And the sinners who watched from the dance floor
Demanded their share of our God

How I loved you forever and ever
As I sang the song Sweet Adeline
So we waltzed to the tune that was silent
But our steps could not keep the time

Ah we danced to a jig that was broken
As the candles burned low in the night
From the wax of each candle we moulded
An effigy golden and bright

Then the effigy stood on a bar stool
And recited the mantra of pain
Then to all of the fools who would listen
It recited her mantra again

Now our feet they are bloody and swollen
As the music continues to play
We have danced every year of forever
We have danced for not even a day

Let me bid you farewell for the evening
As the partners continue to change
And they play Adeline everlasting
Before turning over the page

Smile

Smile profoundly,
as fools
demand
compensation
for whittling
their time away,
like scrimshaw
on bone.

1 priority,
with no life
to spare
except…

Working
towards
the end.

The Canadian Solution

As I ran to find the morning
Where the sleepless lady cried
Of the passion of our music
Leaving sorrow when it died

Yet the woman I'd deflowered
Sewed an old Quebecer gown
As she looked up from the stitches
So my love became her frown

But the next thing I remember
It was thirty years ago
When I sang how much I loved you
As you warned me I must go

Will I dream this dream forever?
Just to wake up in the night
See my candle burning lower
When it used to blaze so bright

Now the maiden of my fable
She was beautiful and wild
Such a woman when I loved her
When I left became the child

I Read The Eulogy At Your Final Gathering

I read the eulogy at your final gathering.
Words written on white paper,
contrasting the dark suits of your sombre guard-
who stood silent and dignified vigil.
Hard to understand why we could never share.
But you said nothing.

I had prepared a short verse,
only forty-five years long,
and in my best oratory delivered it to you.
Tears blossomed like regret,
dripping from moon faces that had travelled far,
but had fallen short in your estimation.
But again you said nothing.

Afterwards we sat around our talking pots,
and spoke of the older times.
I think your name was mentioned, but without intention
we skipped over the issue,
and carried on with our polite but pointless conversation.
But again you said nothing.

Much later I recalled the last smile you gave me.
I had thought your suffering might be too much.
Strange that you seemed tranquil and enlightened,
and I heard you then.
Though again you said nothing.

All We Are Is A Broken Promise

Let me bury all my sorrow
Collected through the years
Then lay atop a wreath of words
That sounded insincere

Then take away my pen and ink
And cast them to the sea
But as the moon commands the tides
Lies flow on back to me

Dismantle all my weapons
But leave this soldiers gun
To keep away the hounds of truth
Surrounding everyone

Ah but if my work is over
I'm not afraid to cry
The harlots and the valiant
Must give love one more try

Caught Inciting Poetry

Caught inciting poetry,
forcing penance to paper,
breaking my life into
manageable portions
easy consumption.
Red say's,
it means what?
Well pardon if the
the meaning is obscure,
look for your own truth.

I don't work in code
but it's no secret
that everyone
should know
about you.
But now
just too tired,
after being so
put upon...

Beyond the call of beauty.

Distance

I long to make this spirit sing
As you did at the start
But fate has taken everything
So many life's apart

You cast me to the morning sun
Cold sorrow eats my heart
And blessings vanish one by one
So many life's apart

But years have gone to testify
The practise of your art
So nothing new will rectify
Our many life's apart

Envelope worker sealed his own fate

Envelope worker sealed his own fate.
I smiled at the intended pun,
but not the consequences
this gentleman had found himself contemplating.
I suppose he only had the world to blame,
as I have blamed the world over again.

The bus driver grins and proudly declares,
you're my only passenger today
It's your disposition my friend.
I have observed people who have a kindly nature.
My shopkeeper is kindly,
and enquires of my health,
as he hands over my favourite brand
of smoking kills.

I leave the driver to consider my statement,
and continue to ignore my journey.
I turn to the next headline.
Fishermen win lottery and push out the boat.

Right Of Way

Though her flight had long departed
To another empty space
And her single minded stubbornness
Was painted on her face

But her dreams of love forever
They could never satisfy
All the men that she had wanted
All the men who said goodbye

O the times that I had asked her
Why she fell in love so fast
And the answers that she gave me
Were buried deep within her past

Yet I know how she has hungered
For the words she never heard
As I lived that life before her
And I've told her what I've learned

You will only seek the open heart
The one you know is true
You will only seek the lonely soul
The one who's just like you

Resurgence

You told me, I was
always at my
best in the
dead of
night.
Words
that where
profound,
with musical
accompaniment
made us weep.

Oh how you tested me
with questions on
sincerity, until
with relief,
dawn broke,
and we slept off
the intensity of our
sexual reassurance.

Something Stalks Me In The Dark

Something stalks me in the dark,
my ego is hunting again.
No longer satisfied with the rotten
morsels of life's conquests,
he craves more.
Oh I denied him so many times,
but his appetite becomes ferocious
and no one is safe.
For pity's sake...
do not feed him

Where The Silent Ones Speak

The grave where every stranger rests
There lies an echoed soul
Beneath the wilted flowerbeds
They sleep where truths are whole

Oh friend please come and walk with me
And hear of all they tell
The lessons learned from lives before
Where fossil bodies dwell

You see the stones engraved with pain?
But markings never speak
About the love's who came and went
Those hearts that never sleep

And if you see a pulse sometimes
Or swelling in the ground
That undulates and permeates
The silence all around

Then let us kneel before each plot
Our ears pressed to the soil
And eavesdrop on the lives that were
Attached to mortal coil

I hear the crying of a girl
Who died while giving birth
The hour set upon the stone
Departure from the earth

But when I take a closer look
The name inscribed is worn
Though I can see the time she died
Was right when I was born

So now I'll listen carefully
As if afraid to pry
To hear the soldier calling me
Who was prepared to die

From Bunker Hill to Valley Forge
We always fought with pride
But heed these words I tell you son
Use Freedom for your guide

And as I pause to read his name
So plain for all to see
It was the very same one that
My Father gave to me

Be still to all who feel the wind
It stirs the restless black
Wild horses gallop in the night
To bring each rider back

One by one, ten thousand more
And with each final breath
Another's born, another dies
As birth begins with death

Now when at last we turn our backs
On souls who were so dear
Whose voices keep on calling us
And beg us to stay near

But hand in hand we walk away
To plan a life that's true
Yet always carry memories
Of hearts that we once knew

Savages

From the people I have suffered
To the things I blew away
With the thought I'd never need them
Or the notion they should not stay

But the friends who stood beside me
Were not anchored in the past
With the ones who I abandoned
And the ones who moved on last

So I make this sacred warning
Should you ever stand to near
Know my heart is like a rapier
With an blade that's forged in fear

Should you ever feel the longing
To take hold this precious thing
Just beware its sharpened edges
And it's vicious lethal sting

Leonard Said

Leonard said,
I am content.
Is this the end?
of my life in art.

Must happiness
hinder articulation?
Light heart
overcome
dark dreaming.

I sleep
at your breast,
like a child
walled up
from pain.

But alas Janis
you must leave,
again
and
again
and
again.

Martha Said

Martha said that I could love you
It was spoken from the heart
And in that misty moment
I knew this was the start

How We walked that road to Heaven
Where I kissed her stocking feet
Prey don't tarry there my love
My lips they are so sweet

But my love I am a sinner
Yes but sinner come inside
And fall into my soft embrace
My heart is open wide

So I spent the night in heaven
And I loved her O so true
Then when at last I said farewell
With Martha I love you

Old Friend

It's been so many years now
I can't believe you tried
To put so much behind you
Of how you schemed and lied

You said you where a player
You said you had it planed
I've seen that all before my friend
I've seen that empty hand

And now your here to tell me
You thought I was the best
A pillar to admire
Don't think I sat that test

But the women that you courted
Where lovers good and true
But you never really loved them
The way that they loved you

And here we are again my friend
That's just how you call me
But things they change forever
And now I really see

Just One A day

See; said my physician,
told you I could cure
you of poetry.
Old black spot
has shrunk
to a tiny
dot.

Thoughts On Love, And Other Things

So he picks up his marker
To highlight the line
That all men are holy
All women divine

But the thoughts that he'd written
Where tainted with pain
He tried to ignore them
They followed again

So he chained up his longing
And no one could find
The key to unlock them
From deep in his mind

Now he's watched from the window
As birds disappear
Another wrong season
Another bad year

But through every long winter
He fashions his tools
To paint out of darkness
And write about fools

Pigeons

I laughed
when you
fed pigeons.

But what
would become
of them
should you
ever leave.

Yet like
the pigeons,
I always
come back
for more.

Winter

You found me in my abstract room
Where metaphors delight
Yet now I sit and worry fate
Into the screaming night

I wrote about your freezing heart
In ways I can't explain
And sang about the vultures song
When I was nearly sane

I lost you in my cursed embrace
Confused to let you know
Why crushing petals of a rose
Can symbolize the snow

I loved you almost everyday
Except when you were here
But ink could never dull the pain
Nor passion melt the fear

So now my love the time has come
When I must let you know
Why crushing petals of your rose
Must symbolize the snow

Ticking Clocks

Ticking clocks
disturb me.

Not because
they remind
me of my
mortality,
or times
past with
redundant
regrets.

It's just...

Ticking clocks
disturb me.

One Legged Man

One-legged man,
himself confined,
swore with profound eloquence,
his mind understated.

Yet language not withstanding
our lady's feelings,
locked in concise English,
was all he said on the subject.

Hope

Hope
Without despair
Despair
Without knowledge
Knowledge
Without understanding
Understanding
Without faith
Faith
Without God

Could all this mean nothing?
Then we find Bethlehem.

How Long Shall I Kneel

How long shall I kneel,
on you're eggshell floor?

Asking for sentence
      Asking for mercy
Begging for nothing
      Begging for something
Wanting to love you
      Wanting to hate you
Needing to hold you
      Needing to let go
Desperate to say so
      Desperate to say no

How long shall I kneel,
on you're eggshell floor.

The Devils Excuse Me

I crept upon a moonlit glade
To lay your bones to rest
I've brought along the devils spade
It suits this job the best

I start to dig then shed a tear
My love she is no more
I'll not forget her look of fear
The last look that she wore

So now at last my love has gone
But there have been so many
And I have cherished everyone
Every one he sent me

Cords

Cords,
stretched
across
infinity.
Hair thin,
but never
broken.

In duress,
snaps back,
causing
two splinters
to shatter
on impact.

Broken Scissors

Broken scissors
dulled the edge
of cutting remarks.

Harsh words,
incomprehensible
screaming metaphors,
from a dribbling fool.

Unfinished Work

I no longer like this poem of love.
Its feet have become crippled, and will not
carry the emotion of the piece.
You said it was your best work, but the effort
was lacking conviction and honesty.
Perhaps the blame is in the subject, maybe it
was dependent on something
not within your vocabulary
nor within your heart.

I no longer care for this sentiment.
Written with little due care or attention,
the detail was inconsistent at best.
Once you were gifted, long ago,
but time has beaten you,
forced your hand, and now
you cannot write truth,

I no longer see the merit in this work.
You have unstressed and stressed to breaking point.
You should practice on the meter, ponder on the flow,
and Wonder at the magic of rhyme.

But you are empty now,
and your talent fooled you.
Pity,
I longed to be your masterpiece.

So Softly Falls The Dust Again

So softly falls the dust again
I know where we must go
It's happened all those times before
A place we used to Know

I made you say a promise
The one you'd never keep
But if promises are lasting
They'll only last a week

I made you swear to love me
Just so you never would
You said it was my sacred oath
I never understood

So you fashioned me a burden
That I carry to this day
Ah but burdens are for bearing
Just bearing me away

You Showed To Me The Blackest Rose

You showed to me the blackest rose
That hung upon your skin
Ah but nature had intended
That rose to lie within

You showed to me your darkened soul
Kept secret for so long
But I glimpsed the glowing ember
That one day might burn strong

You showed to me your broken heart
They said I could not mend
I'll take from you this broken heart
For here is mine, dear friend

Monday Night Is Dungeon Night

Monday night is dungeon night
It looks like I'm not free
Maybe you should stay at home
There's something on TV

Tuesday night is bondage night
My evenings all tied up
Think that you should call a friend
Perhaps go down the pub

Wednesday night is latex night
That's stretching things to much
Don't think I can squeeze you in
You know I'll be in touch

Thursday night is spanking night
A sore point through and through
Later we can sit and talk
You know, just me and you

Friday night is swinger's night
I wont be home till late
There's lots of lovely people
I'm sure it will be great

I've nothing on this weekend
A date could be arranged
You think you could be busy?
I say, that's very strange

Let Us Turn Our Life Down Low

Let us turn our life down low,
and recount the distant past.
I have loved so many times,
in so many spaces.
I have stood outside your window,
in the freezing night.
I have cried when they said,
lust must spring eternal.
I have walked my life away,
in the hope that I could hold you.
I have lied to your soul,
so no one else would harm you.
But when the tables turned,
I had taken everything.

His Ambiguous Writings On Love

I knew a poet
who used obscure
metaphor, to justify
untruths about those
he loved.
But as time passed,
each lie was taken
daily, and used to
prop up the illusion
of his invincibility.

I have become Superman,
he would declare.
Yet was concerned
his new found
redemption, would
one day be denied him.

So he took to falling
in love, all over again.
Analysing each experience,
in a scientific study of self
denial. Then one by one
documented the disasters
that would follow.

But at last when each tale
became the essence of
his existence, he recited
them all back to his victims.
And the whole thing would
start over again.

Changes

Moments drift,
washed away
by deed.
Precious for
a time,
they falter,
turn to
concern
later deceit

Death Of A Wish

If these thoughts could make it right
To steal the life we gave
Within the darkness of our souls
Engulfed before it saves

The two of us no more
Shall walk among the dead
We tramped this road before
Behind the ones who bled

Our hearts must surely break
Along this rotten path
We make it to the end
To save the fatted calf

From fires of our souls
The roasting has begun
It shrivels up our flesh
Like fruit left in the sun

I'll lead you by the hand
A gift you gave to me
From the one who only followed
To one who would be free

Lady Of The Flame Red Hair

My lady of the flame red hair
A sunset bright and strong
You lead me where I long to go
Where I can do no wrong

My lady of the flame red hair
Is our love good and true?
No matter if you say farewell
I'll always look for you

My lady of the flame red hair
Now that we are older
Have old times left their mark on us
Or hard times left us colder

My lady of the flame red hair
We are neither young nor old
For the hand of life is on us now
We have ourselves to hold

No Need To Feel Bad

On the day you came to tell me
How your heart had turned to clay
I washed my hands of innocence
In the filth I'd left that day

But your clay became a symbol
That I moulded to my need
So I smoothed down all the edges
Then I turned my mouth to feed

Yet the feast became too frantic
And we soured all the milk
Since we played malicious games
I wrapped your legs in silk

Ah the rules we set were tarnished
Now they rest in hallowed ground
We'll dig them up again my love
And drag them round and round

The Gift

The gift
of flowers,
does not
constitute
admission
of guilt.

Guilt stems
from Intention,
rather than
deed.
My deeds
have always
crawled from
the innocence
of forethought.

The Tales My Father Told

My Fathers yacht was moored
off the coast of Spain,
but we were never invited
to sail on her.

My Mother would often say,
are you visiting on your Fathers
yacht? But Father never donned
his white captains hat, nor cleaned
his deck shoes for the voyage.

Jewels

Strange,
but I don't think you ever criticised me,
though I've deserved criticism.
No judge and jury you.
Your most condemning sentence,
one sugar remember, not two.

Funny,
but you never get angry with me,
or at least you've hidden it well.
Unconditional and true
it's mentioned a lot,
but only practiced by you.

Did You Find Your Christmas?

Did you find your Christmas?
Wrapped in channel 659,
where goodwill comes at giveaway prices,
and the Angel of loneliness insists,
that salvation can be redeemed,
when items returned are exchanged
for unwanted misery, that waits to be
collected in doorways filled with
unwashed dogs and well-fed beggars.

Did you write your list?
scribbled in haste, posted like
the rest of your life, which you judged
to be...OK, blessed for the good
you've never done, and the wrong
no one has suffered.

Did you weep with him?
Others will. Or was it
to impersonal for you to smother
cynicism with facts?

So I hope you find your Christmas,
as I have discovered mine,
under my plastic effigy.

I Poet

And so it came full circle,
converged once more with hope.
Displaying my agile heart
for the scrutiny of anyone who
dares.

Ah, but have I not shown you
this before? Those times when
I longed for your company,
only to dismiss you.

Then let me wield my mighty
thoughts, so much more in tune
to those who suffered at my hands,
then suffered the kindness of others.
So lets rejoice, for I have redeemed
myself in my own eyes, and that's the
only thing that matters.

So will you reflect with me?
I who have maligned humanity
for the sake of some clever
prose and catchy rhyme.

Then walk with me,
I will tell you all
there ever was to know,
about this careless man.

Jeanne d'Arc

The morning came as answer
Called to my lady's prayer
Yet night time had devoured
Our maiden sweet and fair

It's true I always craved her
Though never would I tell
The many who had loved her
The many who had fell

Her battle cry we followed
With banner flying high
Heaven wept and angels sang
As she gazed at the sky

But fortune soon arrested
Lancaster brought her down
Staked his claim for blasphemy
Then staked unholy ground

Flame can never purify
Or smoke and ash obscure
This heroine so perfect
This child who was so pure

But now her was is over
Though she has left her mark
And I will always love her
Forever Jeanne d'Arc

Do Not Worry, Just For Today

So we bled the Unknown Soldier
For the ones who knew the score
But the barrels of our weapons
Held no flowers anymore

Then the souls that we abandoned
Cried for mercy from the dark
So we marched for their salvation
With our pipe band in the park

Yet the mothers stood forsaken
As the children walked away
Though they yearned for our protection
We had nothing left to say

For although we came as prophets
Of the unborn and the mild
Are we also called to stand by?
Every lost and unknown child

Found In A Humidor

And so I write to you, my love,
unspoken thoughts that plague my brain.
While others wait for evening dreams,
spinning to restful places,
back and forth to heaven,
I dance with fear of losing you...
Long past days of worry, far into madness,
pacing the floor of the ocean counting steps between,
breathing no air, unable to swim.
An anchorless ship, with arduous task
of camouflage, never revealing
my whole self to anyone.

Though I write, I may never send,
shall I burn these words as prayer?
to indifferent gods, maybe flame will light
these corridors of endless uncertainty,
then become the eternal torch that
burdens this desperate soul.
But I will carry this beacon on high,
and though you are distance,
my light may guide you back.

It's here I'll wait for you, my love.
Hallowed hours spent praying you'll return.
I'm only palsied marrow now.
All that's left, gone dead and numb.
Should I try the unfathomable?
Divulging this inner truth, hoping for
emancipation, freeing all that lies within,
what may come of that?
Should I kneel and weep, professing
I am nothing without you, while you stand
akimbo, amused by my devotion?

Is this waiting a futile thing?
My arousal a fools game?
Lonely among millions to chose from,
yet none measure to your ideal.
Forgive me if this is unseemly,
but my platitudes are a desperate measure,
a last ditch volley of shock and awe,
a strategy for your surrender.
a treatise for your consideration,
a white flag, if all else fails.

Cheap Tricks

You said I should refine the art,
as my longing for you grew
in the most intimate of ways.
Yet the detail was in the devil
and the devil was loose,
as I hung your lantern
on my inexperience.

Did I mention my genius?
Gifted with the ability
to confound and confess.
You knew it for sure,
when I said,
I love you,
but don't rely on it.
Reliance is the
dominion of saints,
and though I am a
religious soul,
I am no cheap peddler
Of that philosophy.

One Day I Will Write

One day I will write
this poem for you.
But I have been selfish
with the use of sugar
coated words, much
preferring darker
intonations, to plunge
my sin into.

I recall you wrote me
a letter, asking why
I preferred my own
council, but it was
not the council of an
equal, more the tolerance
of an old fool I craved.

So cherish these words
I have scratched out,
with the hope that they
may mean something
To you.

Know I have searched
For you forever, but
searching is the only
True thing.

A Little Laid Back

Your words
superfluous
say much
mean little.

I listen
edge forward
feign sympathy...
tell me more
but shut up.

I flow
a song darkly
I am mister smiley
I am bright
like winter sun.

But warmth -

Not today.

A Discourse On Writing Implements, And Lust

I wrote this with a quill you know,
to give it a sense of old romanticism,
and perhaps imbue it with a feeling of Shelley.
    That's Mr Shelley by the way,
not that monstrous woman, so famous for sewing
bits of words together to create a monster.
    Though I have been a monster,
who would argue with that?
    But the monsters quill broke at the tip you see,
leaving a large ink blot that covered your name,
and left a further blot on my already overcrowded
copybook.
    Ah, but I left my spare one in your room,
in case I had need of a tool to impress you with my prose.
Oh I know that's what I call it now,
But I also call it being prepared.

Alone But Never Lonely

My tree fell near your house,
you were...*Cold*
So you butchered it for fuel.
But that old tree and I had seen so much
I had nursed it through the empty winter
I had counted the dying leafs on its branches
I knew the texture of its rotten bark
I was aware of its suffering
I am overjoyed it comforts you now
I am happy your toes are warm
I am delighted your toasting fork has a purpose

The Ambiguity Of Descent

You said my words hurt you,
but I shoot them over your head,
so you would not bleed from the irony.
Oh I know you would prefer, la de da de da
but I spoke of the children,
Dresden Warsaw and Hiroshima,
and you spoke of the scene,
New York London and Paris.

Buddha Days

Oh Lord look outside my window
My metaphor to follow
We're safe and sound inside my head
Far from all that's shaped in sorrow

And should you ask about my life
Buddha days that came to pass
I'll point outside just one more time
And whisper lord, our days wont last

Do you think it's time to make plans?
Step beyond that misting glass
If you and I were not so blind
We would see what's coming fast

Now we look to the horizon
See those ships way out at sea?
Yes there sailing here to take us
But will sailing make us free?

I want to hold your hand forever
For my world is insecure
But if my days are really over
Was my faith so much a cure?

I Always Thought Your Eyes were Lovely

I always thought your eyes were lovely.
A well of secrets, you never truly revealed to me.
How much depth they hold, I could sink forever-
but never want to return to gulp sweet air.
Such despair is mine that I am not yours.

I always thought your smile was lovely.
Lips pursed that question ready, but never asked of me.
Lips I have never kissed, I know are gentle,
but sent to torment me, every time they say-
my love, you are never mine.

I always thought your hands were lovely.
So warm to hold, gentle would be their caress.
Nails polished to perfection, finger tip to tip,
but willing to rip this heart from its home.
But for your part, unready and alone.

I Struggled With Greed

I struggled with greed,
as good times only came
in packs of two,
wrapped like Easter eggs
in golden foil. I fought
the longing. But desire
is oh so subtle, twisting
and turning into pleasing
positions, forcing me way
past the count of ten. Until
at last with blistered hands
I moulded love into a more
manageable form...

And fired it in my killing oven.

You Call Again My frequent Friend

You call again my frequent friend
So eager to report
Licking at the bones of my life
The wounds of my old hurt

O let us speak of mystery
Old songs we never sang
Weeping our old mans lament
For bells that never rang

Lets us sip our chocolate latte
Before we say farewell
I'll give to you my secret smile
That only you can tell

Shall we meet again tomorrow?
I've nothing else to do
We'll walk through endless memories
And talk of nothing new

Oblivion

Was I missing the usual metaphors here?
Words that normally flow unrestricted,

Have become constipated, but don't force
the action, my hero said–

lest you become the legendry hairdo,
dying on the seat of oblivion.

We Try, My Love

I played music
But the tone was downbeat, devastating
You laughed
Claimed it suited my melancholy nature

I cooked dinner
But the feast was drab and pointless
You flinched
Then said it must be an acquired taste

I read poetry
But the theme became lost confused
You wept
And Lied that the words where beautiful

Today I Wore My Sunday Face

Today I wore my Sunday face
I keep it hidden for special occasions
locked in a box under my floor
taken out now and again
dusted down and polished up
I test it in the mirror for cracks
smile this way and that
tilt it to a jaunty angle
like an old fashioned hat

Today I wore my Sunday face
it's looking a little tired I thought
tried to scrub it up last night
could not get that old shine back
I hear there's a sale
can I afford a new one?
been saving for a while
so when I remove the wrapping
there's a nice new smile

In Between Nowhere

Collecting driftwood from the shore
She carves in words with care
Then asking where her thoughts came from
Just in between nowhere

She stole my hearts five thousand times
Accomplished with great flare
And every song and poem sprang
From in between nowhere

Then when at last my aching heart
And soul no longer care
I'll read aloud her words of love
From in between nowhere

I'll tie some chain around this heart
So no one else will dare
Remove it from my resting place
Lost in between nowhere

An Unexpected Turn Of Phrase

Write about the sky,
describe how blue it is.

But the sky is dark,
in the most abstract of ways.

Write about the bird song,
describe its melody.

But the song is flawed,
I can no longer bear to hear it.

Write about the rose,
describe the beauty of its petals.

But the rose is black,
and is painted on skin.

Confession Rips The Heart Asunder

What deep secret do you give shelter to in you're oh so silent head? She asked.

No secret I lied, but the feline had escaped from the bag, and was prepared to run rampage with it's perverse curiosity. I should put a stop to it before she started clawing at things best left unsaid.

Your mind is not yours alone, she accused, and your face has turned traitor, must I drag the creature from you kicking and screaming?

I laid naked and exposed as her fingertips shoot tiny bullets of pleasure and pain. I cried for mercy, but mercy from what? Confess that you love me she demanded. Confess that you are mine.

Oh I resisted as long as any man could, indeed more than many have, then at last spent and exhausted I confessed my sin. Yes I love you, and yes I am always yours!

As always with confession the soul becomes brazen, and I dared to ask in return, do you love me? She gazed into my eyes, kissed my lips and softly Whispered in my ear,

you were too easy.

Aphrodite Gives The Game Away

Shall I love you
with the passion
of a martyr?
Becoming
lost in the
futility of the
moment.

Or should I
at least resort
to the excuse
of a coward?
And declare,
Behold,
I am but a man.

Not Really a Fairytale

You pricked my conscience,
with the subtlety of a sledge
hammer. Pounding my heart,
until I became aware
of my nature.

The despoiler of purity,
the apologist of truth,
the analysis of self-loathing.

I took what was offered,
with the gratitude of a glutton,
and all I gave in return,
a half-hearted apology.

Yet I meet you with the
passion of my words,
as they mingled with
This ill-conceived moment.

You swore you could save
me. But salvation means
redemption, and redemption
is for the redeemable.

How I struggled to grip
the line cast to me, as
you shouted... hold on.

But your calls were lost,
to the ecstasy in which
I sank.

Perhaps A Morsel Of Truth

We laughed
as the humor
faded, and
thanked god
that our
feelings where
inadequate.

But the ocean
you call
our pond,
has a solemn
look,
as I prepare
for the crossing.

We All Should Be So Cursed

As weak as any man,
I call to you, night demon
and beg for torment.
But I have seen you with Samael,
and know you will never be faithful
to only one ideal.

You who carry no original sin,
will eat out the sinner,
like the Vampire,
lusting for the sons of light,
from Babylon to Israel
and beyond.

Ah, but I have heard
you know his name,
and are forever cursed
to lay down you children
for your pride.

No wonder you rage
daughter of Hecate,
creation of Hera,
lover from Adam to
Gilgamesh.

But I know you
only as lovely Lilith...

Looking for a place to rest.

You Know I Love You

You know I love you
But you have forged need
Dressed well for slaughter
Blades honed to perfection
I wait to be the lamb
Eager for sacrifice
But never innocent

The innocent do not know
They are imperfect
As we are perfect
Like beasts
You the predator
I the happy prey
Caught in my own trap

But you know I love you

Torquemada Lay Down Your Burning Effigy

Torquemada, lay down your burning effigy, lest you scorch the Earth.
Quell your fanatical enthusiasm for shaking your fist, and proclaiming-
repent, you are off Gods Christmas list.

Torquemada, release the poets and the artists to their work.
Or rip out eloquent tongues, and chop off long fingered hands.
And let them be silent monks.

Torquemada, will you forgo the new inquisition, so that you may
stamp out the insecurities of faith, with courage, passion and hope.
Or issue your proclamation of waste.

Say what you like

Climb this
mountain
of love
my dear,
oh climb
this mountain
of love.

Anything for an easy life

So I climbed
this mountain
of love
my dear,
oh I climbed
this mountain
of love.

Almost at the summit I lost heart

If I Never See You Again

If I never see you again
The sun will shine
Only to burn me
Rivers will flow
Only to drown in
Birds will sing
But carry no tune
Angels will speak your name
But fall on deaf ears
Music will be composed
To be played badly
Verse will be written
Though carry no rhyme
Dawn will break
To my broken heart
If I never see you again

Do You Have A Moment?

The amazing street coward,
invisible to fake beggars.
Doorways make sneaky hiding
places where researchers grave
my opinion, on existence.

But existence eluded me long ago,
leaving me fit to be tied.
Sustained by only bread and water.

I missed it then, but learned
to watch my back.

On a scale of 1 - 10
how would you score love?

One would be a fool,
then ten times the fool.

Would you agree or disagree
with the following statement.

A lover and his sanity are soon parted.

Hmm

Paddy's Rocket

Paddy dreamt of a rocket
He wanted to look at the sky
So he got some things, like glue and string
All the stuff that would make it fly

For a week and a day he laboured
Locked away in the garden shed
But stopped long enough, for meals and stuff
And occasionally going to bed

Then at last the big day came
Friends gathered to wish him farewell
They'd packed him some lunch, he said thanks a bunch
I'll be back with stories to tell

So he soared way out in the stratosphere
Paddy flew so far into space
But got a sore tummy, and missing his mummy
The tears were wet on his face

Paddy came home with his rocket
He was glad that he'd gave it a try
But when all's said and done, you can't beat your mum
Not even if Paddy could fly

The Mutterings Of A Distressed Poet

When my love became my teacher
So eloquent and wise
She taught me everything she knew
Of how to sever ties

Oh the ties they must be broken
Or chains will drag her down
As my heart becomes her anchor
My love will surely drown

She taught suffering inspires
The price that we must pay
When you find someone to love you
Make sure they never stay

For a soul to be contented
That soul has never shown
The heartache and the loneliness
From one who writes a poem

Dark Fantasies

Dark fantasies
forced my hand
into exquisite action.
I burned heretics
for your approval,
and built ships
so you could
sink them.

But no one came
to save me.
Even you swam by
with a song in your
heart, and the words
on your lips...
Thanks for the good times
Lover.

www.ingramcontent.com/pod-product-compliance
Ingram Content Group UK Ltd.
Pitfield, Milton Keynes, MK11 3LW, UK
UKHW041435180426
11947UKWH00007B/449